FLOORED! SUPERCARS

VIPER

y Jared Gall

45TH PARALLEL PRESS

Published in the United States of America by Cherry Lake Publishing Group
Ann Arbor, Michigan
www.cherrylakepublishing.com

Reading Adviser: Beth Walker Gambro, MS, Ed., Reading Consultant, Yorkville, IL

Photo Credits: © Brandon Woyshnis/Shutterstock, cover, title page; © innova11/Shutterstock, 3; © Brandon Woyshnis/Shutterstock, 4; © The Image Engine/Shuttestock, 6–7; © Hirkophoto/iStock.com, 8; © Agus_Gatam/Shutterstock, 10; © RickDeacon/Shutterstock, 11; © Darren Brode/Shutterstock, 12; © drone.studio/Shutterstock, 13; © Jim West/Alamy Live News, 14; © CJM Photography/Alamy Stock Photo, 16; © Hirkophoto/iStock, 18–19; © Zoran Karapancev/Shutterstock, 20; © Hirkophoto/iStock, 22–23; © UPI/Alamy Stock Photo, 24; © Darren Brode/Shutterstock, 26; © Cal Sport Media/Alamy Stock Photo, 28–29; © Hirkophoto/iStock, 30 (top); © Alexander Davidyuk/Shutterstock, 30 (bottom); © Mackenzie Kilmer/Shutterstock, 31 (top); © Steve Lagreca/Shutterstock, 31 (bottom)

45th Parallel Press is an imprint of Cherry Lake Publishing Group.

Library of Congress Cataloging-in-Publication Data has been filed and is available at catalog.loc.gov.

Printed in the United States of America

Note from Publisher: Websites change regularly, and their future contents are outside of our control. Supervise children when conducting any recommended online searches for extended learning opportunities.

ABOUT THE AUTHOR:

Jared Gall writes about cars and trucks for magazines and websites. He has driven everything from semitrucks and school buses to sports cars and supercars. He has raced off-road buggies through the desert in Mexico and Mercedes-Benzes on frozen lakes in Sweden. He has driven a lot of Mercedes-Benzes, but never an AMG One. His personal top speed is 189 miles (304.2 kilometers) per hour, set while driving a Ferrari.

Table of Contents

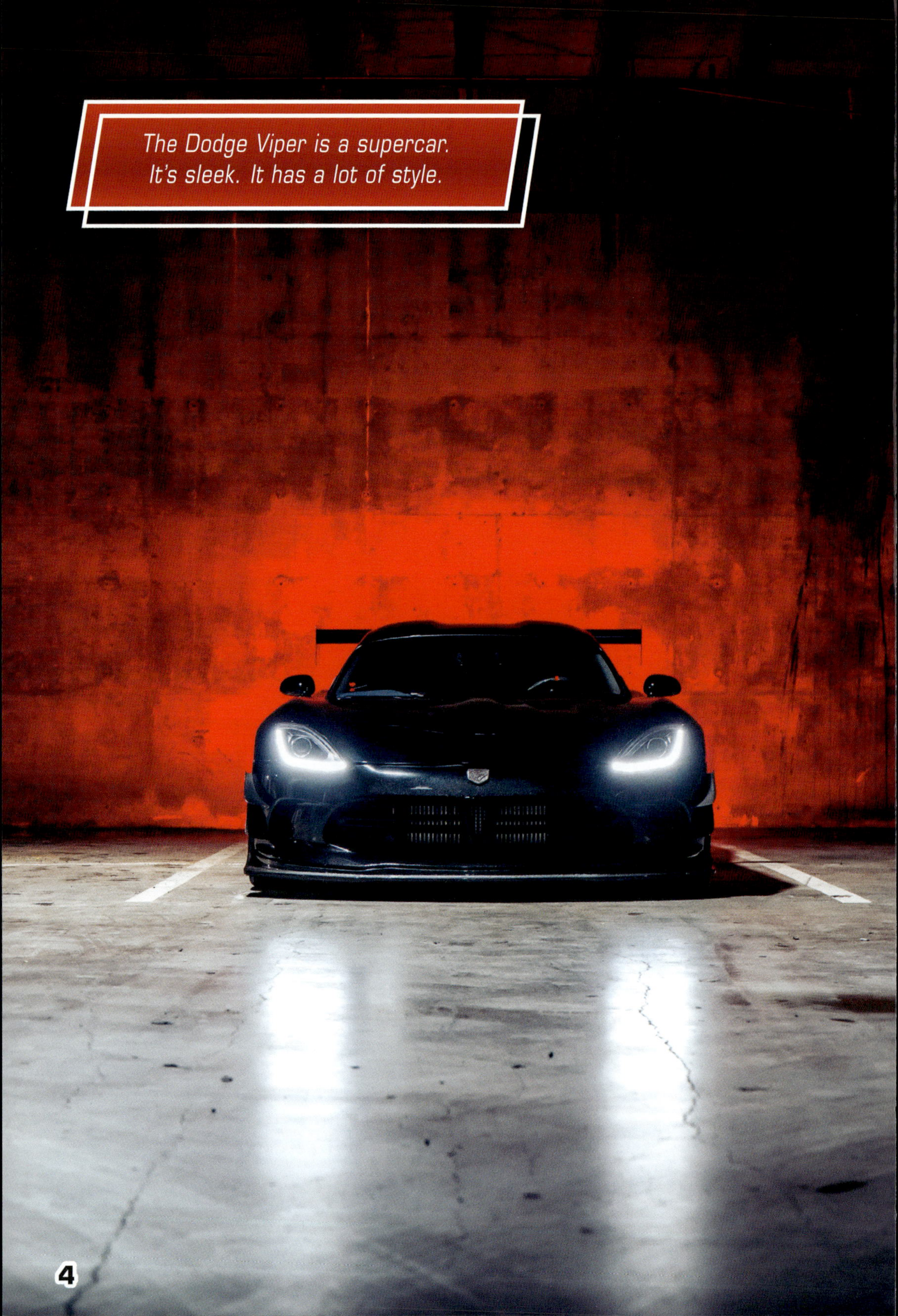

The Dodge Viper is a supercar. It's sleek. It has a lot of style.

CHAPTER 1

Introduction

There are many kinds of cars. They're good at different things. Minivans have lots of space. Whole families can fit. They can ride together to school. They can ride together on vacation. **Sport utility vehicles** are called SUVs. They also have lots of space. They're made to tow heavy things. They tow boats. They tow campers. They also go off-roading.

Sports cars are built to be fast. They're fun to drive. They're small. They're light. This makes them **agile**. Agile means they can turn quickly and easily. They go around corners fast.

Supercars are like sports cars. But they go even faster. Their engines have more power. They're lighter. They can go faster on straight roads. They turn faster. Many are built with special metal. This makes them extra light.

Most supercars sit low. They're close to the ground. This makes them **aerodynamic**. That means they move through air easily. Imagine putting your hand out a car window. Imagine facing your palm into the wind. It would be hard to keep your hand still. But what if you lay your hand flat? It would then be

The Viper is an American car. It's one of the fastest ever.

easier to hold your hand steady. Your hand is more aerodynamic when it's flat. Being aerodynamic makes supercars fast.

Have you ever seen a Viper? Have you seen one on the road? If so, then you have seen a supercar! Vipers are special. Let's learn more!

This is a 2000 Dodge Viper GTS. GTS stands for Gran Turismo Sport. It tells you a car is sportier, fancier, and more rare.

CHAPTER 2

Viper History

It was the early 1980s. Chevrolet had the Corvette. The Corvette was superfast. Ford had the Mustang. The Mustang was fast, too. Dodge didn't make any fast cars. Company leaders wanted that to change.

Designers create cars. They make cars look cool. They make cars safe. They make enough room inside. Cars have to hold people and their things.

Tom Gale was a designer. He worked at Dodge. He designed an exciting new car. His car was low to the ground. It had a long hood. It didn't have a roof. It was a supercar. Gale was inspired by the Ford Shelby Cobra. The Cobra was a famous race car. It was sold in the 1960s. It was the fastest car around.

Gale's boss loved it. The Cobra was named after a snake. Dodge also named their car after a snake. It was called the Viper.

Dodge built a **prototype**. Prototypes are models. Models are needed to figure out what cars will look like. Designers change things. They move things around. They solve problems. The cars that are sold are different from the prototypes.

Dodge was working on a new engine. This engine was huge. It was 4 times bigger than normal engines. It was powerful. It was to be used in a new pickup truck model. Some **engineers** had a better idea. Engineers design things. They build things. They thought the new engine would be better for a supercar.

The Dodge Viper logo is a snake. Viper snakes have venom. They strike fast. Their bites kill.

Truck engines are different from car engines. Engineers needed to change the big engine. Dodge owned Lamborghini in the 1980s. Lamborghini is a famous supercar company. It's made some of the world's fastest supercars. Dodge engineers asked Lamborghini for help.

Dodge showed off the Viper in 1989. This happened at the Detroit Auto Show. Detroit is in Michigan. Auto shows are very important. Car companies from around the world are there. They see what other companies are building. Everyone at the Detroit Auto Show loved the Viper. Dodge decided to build more. The Viper was born.

The Detroit Auto Show is one of the best in the world. It showcases the best in the car business.

The Viper never had exterior door handles.

The Viper was selling before it was ready. The first Viper didn't have a roof. It didn't have side windows. It didn't have door handles. Drivers had to reach inside to open the door. People loved the Viper's design. They didn't care if it wasn't ready yet. They had to have it.

Exhaust pipes control the output of gas. They allow waste to exit. These pipes are at the back of most cars. They get hot. They're hidden. But not on the Viper. The Viper's pipes were on the sides. They looked cool. But people had to be careful getting in and out. The pipes were hot enough to burn their legs. That just made the Viper even cooler. It was loud. It was fast. It was dangerous. It was a supercar.

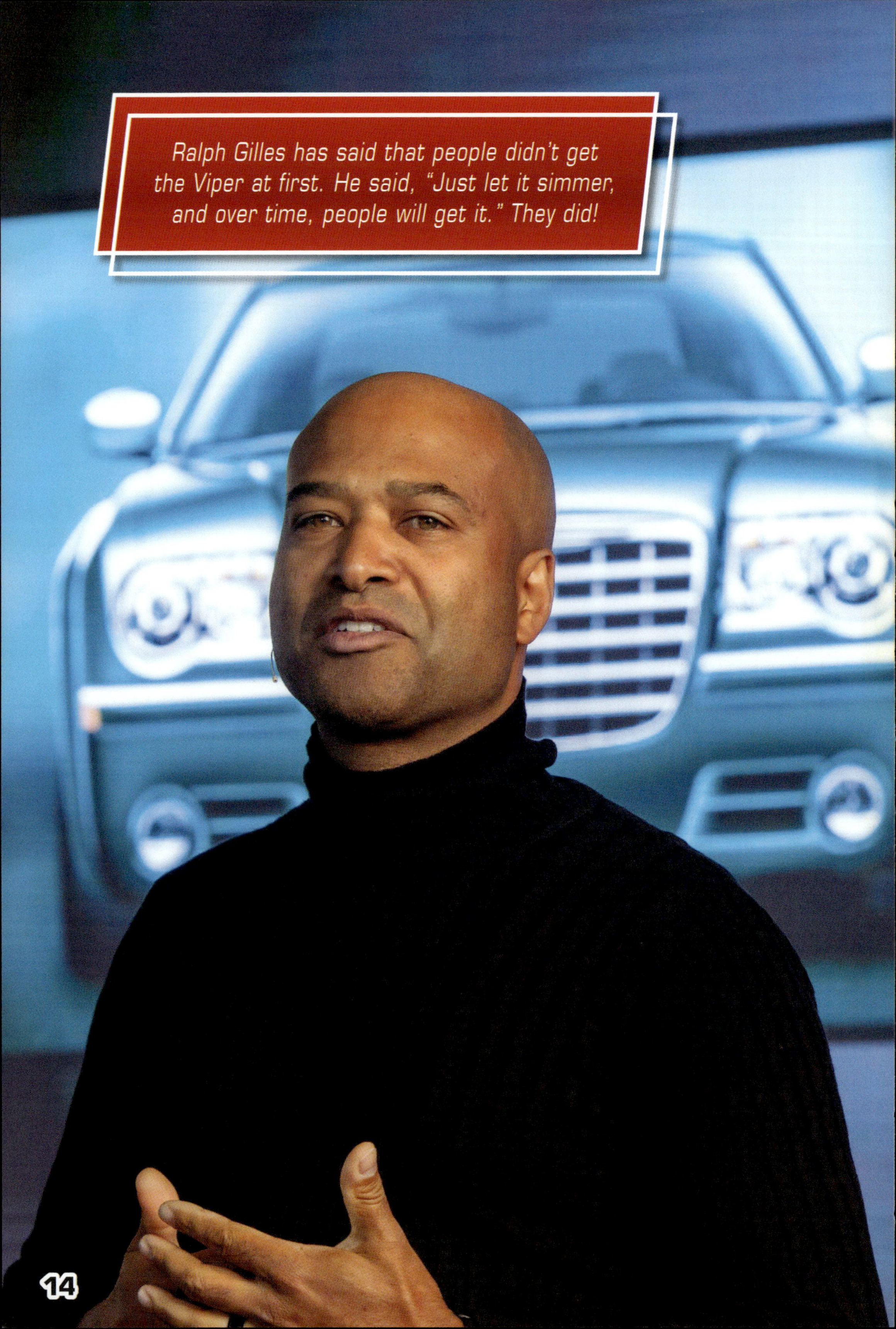

Ralph Gilles has said that people didn't get the Viper at first. He said, "Just let it simmer, and over time, people will get it." They did!

Behind the Wheel

Ralph Gilles is a car designer. He went to college. He studied engineering. But he dropped out. Being an engineer didn't feel right. He had always loved cars. He loved drawing them. He went back to college. He studied design. He got a job at Dodge. He did this in 1992. The first Viper had just gone on sale.

Gilles worked at Dodge for more than 30 years. He helped design many cars. He worked on the Viper. He worked on trucks. He worked on car interiors. He worked on car exteriors. Today, he's in charge of design for Stellantis. Stellantis is a company. It owns Dodge. It owns other car brands. It owns Chrysler, Jeep, and Ram. It also owns Alfa Romeo and Maserati. Those are Italian car brands. Gilles oversees every car design made by those brands.

At Le Mans, drivers take turns driving. They take turns eating. They take turns sleeping.

CHAPTER 3

Viper Evolution

Dodge redesigned the Viper. It did this in 1996. Designers added a top. They added plastic windows that slid open. They moved the exhaust pipes. They moved them to the back of the car. They wanted to make the car safer.

Dodge also made the first Viper **coupe**. It did this in 1996. A coupe is a 2-door car. It has a metal top. A coupe's top doesn't open. Most race cars are coupes.

Dodge decided to race the Viper. The **24 Hours of Le Mans** is a famous race. It's in France. It lasts 24 hours straight. That's a whole day and night! Teams of drivers share a car. The winning team finishes the most laps in 24 hours. The Viper won Le Mans in 1998. It won in 1999. It won in 2000.

The Viper was a very good race car. Dodge wanted to redesign it again. It showed off a new Viper race car. This happened in 2000.

Dodge started selling the new model in 2003. This was the third generation. It looked very different from earlier Vipers. There was a reason for that. Dodge had a new designer. His name is Ralph Gilles. Gilles is Haitian American. He's designed other popular cars.

The Viper gained a more modern look. But it was still very fast.

The Viper SRT 10 had more power than any Viper before it. It went from 0 to 60 miles (0 to 96.6 kilometers) per hour in 3.9 seconds.

The Viper ACR makes more downforce than any other car.

Dodge made the Viper even faster in 2008. It was much more powerful. It could go 202 miles (325.1 km) per hour.

Dodge still raced the Viper. A new version was made. This version was easier for owners to race. It was called ACR. That stood for American Club Racer. The Viper ACR was lighter. It was faster. It had special tires. This helped it go around turns faster. Special brakes helped it stop faster. The ACR also had a big wing. The wing was on the back. It created **downforce**. Downforce is when air pushes something against the ground.

Fast Facts

- The Viper has a rare engine. It is a V10. The only other supercar with a V10 is a Lamborghini.
- Drag racing is a type of racing. Cars go as fast as they can. They do this in a quarter mile. A normal car can go about 90 miles (144.8 km) per hour. A Viper can go 125 miles (201.2 km) per hour.
- The fastest Viper made by Dodge went 206 miles (331.5 km) per hour. Some owners modify Vipers. The fastest modified Viper went 252 miles (405.6 km) per hour.
- The Viper had its own TV show. This happened in the 1990s. The show was called *Viper.* In it, the cops had a Viper. The Viper could change into an armored car. It was used to fight crime.

Imagine sticking your hand out the car window again. Imagine holding your hand flat. It's easy to hold it still. Now imagine tilting your hand down toward the ground. The wind will push your hand down. That is downforce. Downforce pushes a car against the road. This helps it take turns faster.

A Viper ACR can create up to 1,700 pounds (771.1 kilograms) of downforce. That's a lot of weight pushing the car against the road!

The **Nürburgring** is a famous racetrack. It's in Germany. It's a long racetrack. It is 12.9 miles (20.8 km) long. It has many turns. Companies take supercars there. They time how fast their cars go around the track. They compare speeds to other supercars. The Viper ACR's wing helps it go very fast around the turns. In 2011, it raced. It was the fastest street car ever at the Nürburgring.

Ralph Gilles kissed the new Viper after it was unveiled. This happened at the 2012 New York International Auto Show.

CHAPTER 4

Viper Today

Dodge stopped making the Viper in 2010. The Viper cost a lot. People didn't buy a lot of them. The Viper was fast. But other cars were fast, too. The Viper wasn't very comfortable. Other fast cars were more comfortable.

But Viper owners loved their cars. So Dodge started making secret plans. It made a new Viper. It made the fifth generation. Dodge engineers secretly worked on it for 2 years. They made the engine more powerful. Dodge took the car to an auto show in 2012. The car was on a stage. The car was covered with a big sheet. Workers pulled the sheet off. There was the new Viper!

The new Viper was more powerful than ever before. It was faster than ever before. It had **aluminum** parts. Aluminum is a lightweight metal. The new Viper also used **carbon fiber**. Carbon fiber is light, too. Aluminum and carbon fiber are costly. That's why most cars aren't made from them. But the Viper needed to be fast. And being light made it fast.

Dodge made an ACR version of the new Viper. The wing was even bigger. It made more downforce. This Viper could go even faster around turns. Dodge employees took it all over the United States. They drove it on 13 different racetracks. They set records. The Viper was the fastest street car to drive on all 13 tracks.

The 2017 Dodge Viper was the last Viper ever made.

Cost of Ownership

MODEL	PRICE
2024 Toyota Camry	$27,500
2024 Honda CR-V	$31,000
2024 Ford F-150	$39,000

MODEL	PRICE
Dodge Viper	$119,709.96*
Dodge Viper ACR	$160,783.15**

**adjusted for inflation in 2024; was sold for $52,000 in 1991*

***adjusted for inflation in 2024; was sold for $121,395 in 2014*

But Dodge didn't go back to the Nürburgring. It's too costly to travel there. American companies are farther away. They have to cross an ocean. They have to pay for travel. They have to take teams. They have to take their cars. They transport cars on ships or planes.

But Viper owners wanted to go to Germany. They wanted to see how fast the new model could go. Many of them put their money together. They raised more money. In 2017, they had enough money. They took the Viper to Nürburgring!

The Dodge Viper GTS has a top speed of 206 miles (331.5 km) per hour.

Vipers appeal to many Americans. They have personality. They're bold. They're dangerous. They're hard-working. They're fighters. Remember, the first Viper didn't even have windows. And it still became one of the world's fastest cars.

Vipers have many fans. Owners formed a club. There's a Viper Club of America. It started in 1996. This proves how special Vipers are. People love them. What's not to love? Vipers have a cool name. They have a cool look. They're just cool.

Timeline of a Legend

1989
The Viper is presented at the Detroit Auto Show.

1992
The Viper is available for sale.

1994
Viper TV show starts.

1996
Second-generation Viper is introduced.

1998
Viper wins Le Mans for the first time

2003
Third-generation Viper introduces new styling.

2008

Fourth-generation Viper is the first to go 200 miles (322 km) per hour.

2013

Fifth-generation Viper is offered only as a coupe.

2017

Dodge stops making Vipers for good.

2017

The Viper goes to Nürburgring. It sets its fastest lap time.

Find Out More

BOOKS

Cruz, Calvin. *Dodge Viper SRT.* Minneapolis, MN: Bellwether Media, 2016.

Zatz, David. *Dodge Viper: The Full Story of the World's First V10 Sports Car.* Poundbury, UK: Veloce Publishing Ltd, 2021.

WEBSITES

Search these online sources with an adult:

A Brief History of the Dodge Viper | Carhub

Dodge Viper | Academic Kids

Glossary

24 Hours of Le Mans (twen-tee-FOHR OW-uhrz uhv luh MAHNZ) a famous endurance race in France

aerodynamic (air-oh-dye-NAA-mik) able to move easily through the air

agile (A-juhl) able to change direction quickly

aluminum (uh-LOO-muh-nuhm) a very lightweight metal

carbon fiber (KAR-buhn FYE-buhr) a very strong, lightweight material

coupe (KOOP) a 2-door car that usually seats 2 people

designers (dih-ZYE-nuhrz) people who create plans for cars

downforce (DOWN-fors) a downward aerodynamic force

engineers (en-juh-NEERZ) people who design and build things

exhaust pipes (ig-ZOST PYEPS) pipes that release gases from the car engine into the air

Nürburgring (NUR-ber-gruhng) a famous racetrack in Germany

prototype (PROH-tuh-tyep) an original model of something that shows how it will work

sport utility vehicles (SPORT yoo-TIH-luh-tee VEE-uh-kuhlz) vehicles designed to be used on rough surfaces but often used on city streets; also called SUVs

supercars (SOO-per-kahrz) cars designed to go faster than other cars

Index